A Snobby Girl's Guide to Dealing with Cancer

Surviving Cancer with Humor, Grace and Style

MAUREEN MILES BUCCI

ISBN: 0578134063
ISBN-13: 978-0578134062

DEDICATION

This book is dedicated to my husband Tom, with whom I battle cancer and live my life. Speaking of which, I owe my life to 'Team Cancer' of Main Line Gynecologic Oncology, under the direct supervision of Drs. David O. Holtz, Albert S. DeNittis and staff. My treatment was undeniably the best anyone could ever hope to receive. I am forever grateful. May God hold them in the palm of his hand. And in memory of Slicks the Cat, who was by my side during this entire ordeal. He began his journey to heaven four days before I received the news that I was clear of cancer cells. May God bless your little paws. You performed your tasks well.

CONTENTS

FORWARD

WOW! Game Changer: I've been diagnosed with cancer. Not the pink ribbon cancer everyone knows about but the teal/peach/purple kind. Ribbon colors designate a type of cancer – teal ribbons for ovarian, peach for endometrial, and light purple, now an inclusive color for all gynecological cancers. Ovarian and endometrial cancer claim the lives of 15,000 American women per year; therefore, I hope all of us ladies will keep this in mind when it's time to donate to the cause. Ovarian cancer is the fifth most frequent cause of death for women. According to the American Cancer Society, 21,980 women will be newly diagnosed in 2014. One out of 73 women are at risk of contracting this disease, and the risk of dying from this disease is approximately one in 100.

The slogan associated with endometrial cancer is *"Listen, it whispers,"* since the symptoms are often silent because they're masked by aging and menopause. I am *not* a medical professional, but please heed this piece of advice: if you notice any signs of unexplained bleeding or a constant bloated feeling, mention it to your doctor. We tend to dismiss these symptoms as normal but they could be a warning of something potentially life-threatening.

I would like to be perfectly clear that this is not a *self-help* book; it is fun and a little mean...pure and simple. It is not for the faint of heart, nor is it cutesy, apologetic or nice. The information presented is brutally honest and addresses some of the dirty little secrets associated with life during cancer treatments. It is a compilation of my experiences and those of others I've personally met during this time.

I'm a people-watcher and I listen intently. My story is like so many others who, sadly, must face this disease alone or with one special care giver. I don't have a psychology background or any other credentials to give advice except good, old-fashioned common sense, tempered with the knowledge of heartache, and the ability to laugh at life. I'm writing for the sole purpose of helping others deal with the life changes that inevitably come about after diagnosis. I hope my story can help both the women who are diagnosed and the people who care about them. Now *Giddy Up!* We're going for a ride.

1. MY JOURNEY BEGINS

As a 58 year-old female, I have met all kinds of women. With few exceptions, I've judged most to be shallow. But ever since my cancer diagnosis, my outlook has changed. I am much less likely to judge. Once upon a time, whenever I'd see an apparently able-bodied and perfectly capable woman parking in a handicapped spot, I'd think to myself, *"She should be grateful she doesn't need that spot and let someone more deserving have it."*

Now I realize that outward appearances can be quite deceiving; the woman may look fine, but she could be experiencing excruciating pain as a result of a recent chemotherapy treatment. These days, I offer the benefit of doubt before judging. You see, I too look very healthy outwardly, but know the ache of muscle and bone pain – the silent suffering no one wants to experience.

As I journey through my new life as a cancer patient, I see the world through the eyes of someone who struggles. I'm also in the unfortunate position of having to watch my care givers try to absorb my suffering. Although it is futile, they would give all they have to take some of my pain away. Seeing their effort first-hand, I believe that the care-giver may suffer as much – if not more – than the patient.

I perceived my cancer as an opponent, a worthy adversary not to be taken lightly. I saw it for exactly the monster it had become, and I was willing to take up the challenge to defeat what was slowly killing me. I realized early on that the battle would be fierce and that I might have to surrender at times – but only to afford myself enough time to regroup and face another day. I have differing emotions when it comes to the cancer fight.

Part of me wants to believe we can control our destiny, while another side relents and insists that cancer will do what it wants to do, and we are powerless to stop it. At best, we can only subdue it for a while. While the scales tip over to the side that believes we have control, my heart also aches for those who succumb to the disease. I continue to think this over daily. I wish I had an answer but the truth is, cancer really does not discriminate; it attaches itself to whoever crosses its path. I pray for the day the roads split to allow us to travel the healthy path of life without having to fight the monster, cancer, which has taken a new direction – far away from humanity, where it can no longer harm anyone.

I've been told that my story is extremely negative. First of all, I'm alive and living each day as a new and improved product, and that is the most positive achievement a cancer patient can experience. Secondly, unless you've gone through it, please don't judge. This book is geared toward survivors: people who are battling and those who wait every six months to hear if they have to go back into treatment. It is not for the easily offended. My original purpose was an attempt at nasty satire but as I looked around and saw the pain and stress, I decided to tell the truth as we patients see it. The diagnosis of cancer is an ominous event, so by all means, laugh at what I've written here. If a particular someone or situation sounds familiar, laugh about it. It heals.

Ok, now that I have written my disclaimer, my apologies in advance of the following pages; I am moving into the realm of cancer reality.

Onto my instructions about how our friends and family members should behave. I'm sure by now you're probably asking yourself who I am to set the rules. Well, I am as insignificant as the rest but someone has to speak for those who are struggling to maintain a balance between disease and everyday living. As a society, we have really dropped the ball. People are so obsessed with public displays of sympathy, they forget there is a real human being with skin and (probably not much) hair behind the heartbreak of a cancerous disease.

My feelings may be totally different from others. That being said, it's my book and my story. I am hoping it relieves the pain of loneliness to many facing the same circumstances. And because I'm a snob, it's all about *me!*

2. IT'S OKAY TO CRY

No one sees my tears or hears the sobs, but that's the way I wanted it. I wasn't asking for sympathy, nor was I expecting any. All I knew was that I'd fight this battle with my husband by my side; he was my back-up and that was it.

But I made a big mistake believing a strong leader would emerge and organize my household and life into a manageable place of healing. It doesn't happen! You're on your own. This will appear quite harsh, but alas, it is the norm for many people. I chose to elaborate on this because it is important to be prepared.

For the first few weeks, you are the story of the day, but then the trips to the hospital begin and the trials of the journey begin to emerge. When you have a good day, make some extra food because there will most likely be days when you're just too tired to cook. Don't mislead yourself into thinking your life will remain the same as it was before you started chemo because it probably won't.

But this part saddens me the most: Don't be surprised when friends forget you. They'll justify their actions and often blame *you* for their lack of concern. They may go on about how busy they are or offer some other excuse for not helping. When they describe their hectic schedules in detail, they're essentially letting you know you are no longer a priority. Therefore, it's best to move on and avoid conflict. You'll only hurt more after they reprimand you that you should have asked for help.

Whatever you do, don't confront them. You have neither the strength, nor the time to pursue this trivializing turmoil. Doing so will only weaken you at a time when it's critical to place yourself at the top of the care list. Make this the time of your life when you are on a pedestal and live accordingly. That being said, you will probably still have to climb down occasionally to clean the counter and vacuum the carpet as part of living a normal life.

Now onto my journey through the different personalities I've had the pleasure of knowing during this drama. I begin with the ever-insistent….

3. THE FRIENDS MEDICAL ASSOCIATION

What an enlightening experience it is to be diagnosed with cancer and then find out most of your friends are closet doctors! I call them *"Friend Docs."* They know everything, beginning with the classic question, **"Do you have a good doctor?"** I've been tempted to answer "*No*, not the best." I must emit an aura of stupidity. Of course I would naturally seek out an adequate doctor when my life is at stake! Upon realizing you are satisfied with your medical selection of doctors, the never ending questions and complaints begin.

Why didn't your Dr. perform this test? Everyone knows this test is important, and I can't believe he hasn't sent you for one!

Answer: "When he pulled the cancer out of my body it was a good indication I'd need treatment. Also as a side note, the pathologist agreed. But I do understand your concern that time could have been used better by undergoing this unnecessary test. My mistake! *Of course* I understand you have my best interest at heart when you interrogate me concerning my choice of medical care. I'll be sure to relay your comments and concerns to the doctor at my next appointment."

But wait, there's more.

"Well, if you have to get cancer, this is the best one to get."

Really?! Let me inform you, there is no such thing as a "good" cancer! They are all horrible diseases, but I will allow you to feel this way if it eases your conscience. This uniformed proclamation is a great comfort as you return home from your first experience as a human receptacle for strange and bizarre chemicals, but I guarantee you, one of the Friend Docs will make this statement.

"You got through your first bout with chemotherapy fairly easily so radiation treatment should be a piece of cake. There are no side effects associated with radiation."

"Really!!!"

I've devoted a whole section on the non-existent radiation side effects but for now I will concentrate on chemotherapy. When I say I was able to tolerate the side effects of chemotherapy I mean I was *able to tolerate them.* I never said I felt great or that I wasn't ill or that the pain wasn't unbearable at times. I said it was *tolerable.* I sometimes wonder if those who choose to suffer this pain in private frighten those who don't understand. They want to believe it's an easy fix, but they're informed enough to know the dire consequences that result from having foreign chemicals released into the blood stream. They know it's going to cause havoc.

Yet if you resist their suggestions or try to explain how your situation is different, you will feel their wrath. They will give you a daily dose of how insignificant you truly are. You might be the one undergoing treatment but they certainly know much more about this than you could ever imagine. You see, their friend's sister's husband went through the same thing. Again, *really?* When did he have ovaries removed?

I'm spending a little more time on this group than I should but let's face it, is this not amusing?

And to add to the wealth of knowledge they have gained, they'll insist you try this 100-percent guaranteed cure they found on the internet. If you eat seaweed and cat food in addition to a supplement they'll sell you for $19.99, it will cure your cancer. *So-and-So* did it and their doctor cannot understand why the tumor disappeared. He didn't want to tell the doctor about his new diet supplement because he just wouldn't understand.

REALLY?!

And what if it *doesn't* work? I guess I'll just die. Seems a little too risky to me.

Keep this thought in mind whenever you run into a Friend Doc:

They Don't Know What They Don't Know.

Yet they think they know it all. I will guarantee you someone will say "Don't worry about losing your hair; it's only hair," or the ever popular "It'll grow back." Ugh! It is okay for them not to worry because it's *your* appearance that will be changed and not *theirs*. I cannot stress enough the advantage of preparing yourself for these moments…and there will be many.

I did start answering these people sarcastically because quite frankly they are ill-mannered. As such, I felt they should be treated accordingly. So if you want to set things straight from the beginning, explain to them that it *is* a big deal. Be prepared though: they'll argue the point and tell you how irrelevant hair is because the important thing is that you do get better and *blah, blah, blah*!

When you add the insult of baldness to a body that may have lost breasts and is sporting tattoos from the radiation treatment or scarring from an operation, it is a very big deal. If you looked in the mirror and your reflection showed you what we see, you might think twice about making ignorant comments. Which is why I repeat, *they don't know what they don't know.*

I would like to take this opportunity to ask all of those who have been lucky enough to escape the pains of cancer-related drugs to refrain from giving their opinions regarding our healing. You have no idea what we are dealing with, so you should act appropriately. Your opinion is hurtful and confusing since our experiences are poles apart.

∞ Prescription for Friend-Docs ∞

Whenever I go out in public, I wear a wig and an appropriate amount of make-up to cover my gray tinge so I appear normal. Most women dealing with cancer do the same, so why not take the patient you know out for some retail therapy instead of visiting their home? Outside stimulation is very good for the mind and we *can* function normally. Although marathon shopping is a great way to spend a Saturday, even just a few hours would really spike our attitude. The mall is probably not the best idea but how about taking your friend to the wig shop or the cosmetic counter?

Do something different; go hat shopping with us. It really is fun and you may find yourself looking toward a new look for yourself. We *Gray Smoothies* love finding anything to make us look normal, and we could use the advice as to fit and appearance.

A hat boutique is an awesome place to lose yourself. Every hat is an escape. My child's imagination was reignited as I tried on Little Lady hats, Victorian hats and brimmed hats of our day. Cancer forces you to look at life differently, but it doesn't mean it can't be enjoyable. So why not call and set up a "Hat Date" with your friend? I can guarantee you'll forget about your own troubles for a little while. Step out of the cancer phobia box and do something unusual. They say a leopard doesn't change his spots but you can always add a cheetah hat to the mix....

∞ Like Share, Blah, Blah, Blah ∞

Some self-appointed experts believe the world can be saved by clicking "Like" or – if it's really special – "Share." I have put these people into the *"One-Second Category."* They are way too important to spare more than one second of their valuable time to convey their support. Keep those close who have the kindness in their hearts to ask, "How are your legs feeling?" or "Can I get you something from the store?" These are the things that matter most. These are the people who take meaningful action to help ease your pain, even though their efforts are not posted on a social networking site.

I actually gave up posting any information at a very early time. I used a story-telling version of my status on social media because I believed it was appropriate.

As I read through the daily complaint postings including *Fx#@ My Life* (FML), *I hate my job*, *Life isn't fair*, *My children are the best but all of the others have problems*, I was tempted countless times to offer to trade with them. I became acutely aware of the importance of the daily routine when it was suddenly removed from my life. The subtraction of the minimal tasks – such as washing your hair – creates an upheaval and a void. I remember many occasions when I wished it didn't take so long to style my hair but because it was an everyday task I was accustomed to, I sort of missed it. Still, I made the decision not to offer the trade since everyone knew I'd be fine and should just enjoy lying on the sofa watching television. You see, in their eyes, *I* was the lucky one.

But to balance out some of the negative, I'll add that the ordinary becomes awesome when you can no longer enjoy the trivial. I like styling my hair now. There are times when I leisurely wash and condition it and treat it like a prize. I know I'm jumping ahead but when I went for a haircut after being bald for a few years I cried. The trivial and mundane really is amazing.

∞ Becoming a Human Solar Panel ∞

The first time you see yourself as a balding woman, you cry. And you cry for days. No one else sees this, but you feel it. And everyone you run into asks the same unending question: *"Did you lose all of your hair?"* Which is always followed by "Oh, it's not a big deal, and besides it comes back even better."

Really!!!

I guess since it's not your hair it is okay, but how exactly do you know it comes back better?

When I discussed the issue with the medical staff, they told me I would lose my hair within three weeks of my first treatment. They were spot-on. I was *never* told my hair would come back better or different.

Actually, when I told my doctor my hair was growing back he was happy. For some reason, there is a large group of people who regard chemotherapy as a follicle treatment. It is not, so please refrain from relaying such nonsense. We *Smoothies* know the truth. Yes, I've adopted the name *Smoothie* for my balding head. Since I have to live with it, I might as well give it a cute name.

And while I am on the subject of hair loss, please refrain from sending me pictures on social media of bald women and bald cartoon characters. It is not the least bit comforting to know the cartoon characters "support the cause" by parading around without hair. To put it in perspective, they are *cartoon characters*. Please put yourself in our place when you open your Facebook page and see bald women staring back at you with a little caption that reads "I support you." No, you don't. You are displaying public sympathy, which I have never asked for. I have not changed my profile picture to show my current status of Smoothie.

I wear a wig when I am in public, and sometimes a hat over that because my head gets cold. The Friend Docs forgot to tell me about how hair keeps your head warm. Note to self: Friend Docs make mistakes too.

There is physical as well as psychological pain involved with hair loss. The first sign I was losing my hair was scalp pain. The only way I can explain it is to describe how after you bump your head, it leaves a lump that's painful to touch. My scalp was a bit red and sore right before the hair would fall out. It was very unpleasant; however, I used it as a sign of other things to come.

If you have long hair, it may be a good idea to shave your head before you experience symptoms of hair loss. I was very surprised to find my hair was breaking off before it began falling out. When I woke up in the morning, I would find an outline of hair where my head was lying. The little cotton pull-on caps they sell are very helpful because they catch the hair and relieve some of the discomfort. You can find these at any wig or hat store. Since you really lose a lot of heat through your head, the caps are soothing. Some kind ladies will sew these for you and leave them in *Chemo Land*, and nurses and other patients will tell you where to find the kindness table.

Feel free to look through everything it has to offer and help yourself. It is amazing how many helpful things are left for your comfort. One night you may be so happy to have a handmade cap for your head, or something else that brings you relief. Which reminds me, this is a great time to say *Thank You* to all the kind ladies who sew, knit or crochet for us.

4. THE TURNING POINT

I am no longer the *Snobby Girl* I once was. I miss her but I've become someone else. I'm not sure who I am yet, but I'm moving ahead.

As I read what I have just written I am laughing. I hope you are too, because we must keep a sense of humor during these times. God has given us the gift of laughter, so use it. Laugh out loud. Somehow the body parts associated with laughing are immune to the chemicals and it feels good.

Now, here are some hard truths from a *real* patient, not a Friend Doc:

❖ You lose all of your hair. People will try and find delicate ways to ask if this includes pubic hair. The answer is yes. I'm not sure exactly why this is such a popular question, but it is, so I've answered it. You can also lose eyebrows, eyelashes, arm hair, leg hair and nose hair. These side effects can really be irritating so prepare for this and buy some soft tissues. The nose hair is an amazing filter we take for granted. Fine particles are not filtered anymore, so you have to be more aware of a runny nose. This isn't pleasant but I'm adding it because the last thing we need is surprise or embarrassment.

❖ Your skin takes on a grey tinge, kind of like the alien movies from twenty years ago. Again I stress: buy cosmetics before you start treatment.

❖ You do not always lose weight; sometimes you gain weight. You may also take on the appearance of a feeding tick or a moving beach ball, or the polar opposite of a stick. We're all different and I know of nothing to combat this one.

❖ A paper cut could take three weeks to heal so you must be very careful with daily chores. This is an area in which we can all use some help.

❖ Hands and feet could go numb at any time.

❖ Chemo-head results in forgetfulness, cloudy thinking, trouble with focusing on tasks and so much more.

❖ Inevitable eyesight problems include dryness and focus issues.

❖ Learn to wear clothing to hide your bruises. I found this to be one of the most difficult challenges. I bruise easily now and walk around with an assortment of black, blue, green and red markings all over my arms and legs. Again, I have no idea how to get through a day without banging into something. Funny how you never notice how clumsy you are until the marks start appearing. All this time I thought I was very poised – ha! Chemotherapy is such a boorish teacher.

As hard as you try, you cannot totally erase that look of having cancer treatment. But I went out and bought new wigs and make-up before I started. It was probably the best decision I have ever made. This way I was able to match my blonde coloring with my foundation and appear somewhat normal. It worked. This is my *Snobby Girl* tip to other ladies in my situation: Go out and shop before your first treatment. Buy everything new and enjoy them because it may be the last time you visit the cosmetic counter for a while.

∞ **Wigs** ∞

Wigs are not so bad these days but they do tend to slip a little or move around when you rest your head against the chair back. Get used to holding your head up straight when sitting.

If your wig doesn't fit exactly the way your natural hair looked, go to a professional stylist who specializes in them. It is truly an art form of its own and most hairdressers do not have the equipment or the experience to trim your wig. Be aware that even in winter, wigs are very hot. I would find myself hiding in a room and taking it off just to get some relief. Honestly, I haven't found a way around this yet. They do make cooling headbands which fit around your head and are supposed to keep your wig in place, but I really didn't receive much relief from them either.

As for wearing wigs in the summertime, I have no suggestions. The cooling bands do keep you a tad cooler but when it's 90 degrees in the shade, nothing is going to keep you comfortable. I started wearing hats but I should warn you that will attract unwanted questions. I've been asked on more than one occasion why I'm wearing a hat in this heat. Despite honestly answering the question, the confrontation continues. "Don't you know they make wigs for that?"

Why yes, I do, but how would you like to walk around wearing what amounts to about two woolen caps in this heat? They just don't get it, so walk away.

And there's another serious issue related to wigs: flammability. Synthetic wigs are flammable so if you're using one, it is extremely important to remove it while cooking, or near an open flame. The woman at the wig shop made me aware of this, but I was surprised to learn how many people don't know. Remove your wig if you have any concerns about being near a flame.

∞ **Eye Glasses** ∞

The first time you try to fit your glasses under your wig is a minor disaster. Pure and simple, they will not fit right. My solution? Get the arms readjusted. I found that if you straighten out the arm so it points straight back, it is a little more comfortable. But, be careful not to straighten too much because they will fall off when you lower your head. I went almost straight with just a tad of a bend to hold them to my ears.

If you're lucky enough to find the right spot on your first try, don't touch them. It is an achievement. Sometimes if your wig moves, the glasses will pop up and then you start over.

It does get much easier with time and practice, but if you happen to wear bifocals, trial and error is your best bet. My eye doctor warned me that chemotherapy affects eyesight. Sure enough, I noticed an unbelievable change in vision, along with constant dryness and irritation. Thankfully, when I finally finished with chemotherapy my eyes returned to their pre-treatment condition, with the exception of extreme dryness.

∞ **Eye Makeup** ∞

Because you are missing eyebrows and lashes, you can get away with wearing extra eye make-up. For some reason, you look so much prettier with added eye shadow. Although I'd never been a fan of heavy eye make-up prior to cancer, I must admit I look so much better when I pile it on. My normal daily routine now includes black liner and three colors of shadow. I save time not having to apply mascara, and I've learned how to draw a pair of eyebrows that look pretty close to normal. If you smudge the brows a bit after you draw them on, they take on a natural appearance.

If an eye pencil leaves a thick-looking line, you can try using dark brown shadow applied with an angled brush. I used this technique and it worked well for me until the brows returned.

These are the only tips I can offer now but it's not uncommon to learn something new from another patient in *Chemo Land*. If you see someone with beautifully done eyes, don't be afraid to ask how they applied their make-up.

∞ Empty Platitudes ∞

"I'm here for you, just ask....except of course if I'm doing something better..."

"If you need anything let me know...."

And the old favorite: "You should have called me, I told you to call me if you needed anything!"

Do you get the sense it's your fault?

Why is it our fault? People ought to realize they should call the patient and offer specific assistance. Once again, allow me to set things straight as to why we won't ask for help: It is the fear of being told "**No**." Yes, it does happen and quite honestly it sucks what little life you have right out of you. You are no longer part of "normal."

In the beginning, you're the flavor of the day. Did you hear, *So-and-So* has cancer? After your first treatment, everyone comes by to see if you've turned into a chemically altered manster (half man/half monster). Then they'll look at you and say, "You're doing really well. No one would ever believe you are going through chemotherapy." That eases their conscience so they don't have to come around or call as often. "No big deal, she's fine."

There's the kick.

After the second treatment, a few still dial your phone number, but most are on their way to the mall – minus the bald woman who wears a wig, with penciled eyebrows and alien skin.

But there is a redeeming factor: the inner strength you develop. I still have no idea where it comes from, but I have it. I am perhaps the strongest one of the bunch.

I've been advised I'm too hard on people because they are just trying to say the right things. I understand that, but this is serious. To those dealing with cancer, paper feelings become irrelevant. If you're sincere about helping out, *just do it*, to use a popular marketing tagline. Call and ask what you can do on behalf of your friend with cancer. I guarantee you the recipient of that phone call will be grateful and smiling.

∞ Pain is Weakness Leaving the Body ∞

Years ago, I learned this technique from a Marine who taught me how to use pain psychologically to become stronger. At the time it was in reference to physical training (PT) but I've found it describes my struggle perfectly now.

When I mentioned it to my *real* doctor, he glanced over to an associate and smiled somewhat. I believe he knew this was true and that I would be taking the pain journey to recovery. I have not changed my opinion with respect to dealing with the pain, and I have no intention of allowing the symptoms and side effects to keep me from achieving the goal. (As an infomercial to the *Friend Docs*, we patients do experience pain.). After my first treatment, I thought someone was sticking hot pokers in my legs. It hurt badly, but I endured by understanding the pain as "One Cell Down." Thereafter, I relied upon this wisdom to reach the day when the weakness would be gone and my body would be strong again.

Friend Docs use the terms, "bump in the road," "small setback," etc. I laugh at this because I know that there is no bump capable of forcing me to reserve a permanent seat on the sofa, or any setback that can keep me from shopping. It is pain that can bring tears to your eyes or may just shut you down altogether as you try to sleep through it. I don't want to overemphasize this point, but these irrelevant sayings are so annoying. We smile and nod, but do you want to know what we are really thinking? Here it is, wait for it:

Stop!!!

They are meaningless statements, totally out of context with what we are experiencing. If anything, it is a giant exasperating pothole that I fell into and I can't seem to figure a way out of. This is a little *Bitch Speak* but it must be said.

Psst....*Know someone who says these things and want to get the point across?* Leave the book open to this page.

∞ Chemo Head and Nausea: Let's Boot and Rally ∞

Chemo Head is good for entertaining Friend Docs who have all the answers. Problem is, those of us undergoing treatment experience this phenomenon and tend to forget the questions. It's actually funny at times, but chemotherapy has a direct effect on the brain, which causes forgetfulness and confusion.

I have caught myself watching a football game and not remembering which teams are playing.

Although the ability to remember comes back quickly, for a second you lose your train of thought and move to a place swirling with bewilderment. The confusion clears up fast but I believe the problem of forgetfulness may be somewhat permanent. I must check with the Friend Docs for confirmation, however (yes, that was sarcasm).

I've also experienced more lasting memory loss. I'll forget where I put things, what I'm doing and what I have to do. It's not unusual for me to walk around with a notebook so as not to forget what was really important. Speaking of which, at print I have lost my notebook.

There was an old song by Lou Reed entitled "Let's Boot and Rally" in which you would drink, vomit and start drinking again. For me, in a comical way, chemo is a little like this. You certainly need a sense of humor and a rallying call. I've adopted "Boot and Rally." No further explanation needed.

A friend and cancer survivor told me about Essence of Orange Oil and its effects on the brain. Somehow it takes away the feeling of nausea. I'm not exactly sure how it works, but it does. At the first sign of queasiness, place a dab under your nose. It smells like an orange peel and the nausea seems to ease up. I've also heard that an orange peel works just as effectively. Essence of Orange Oil can be purchased at a health food store and sells for about $10.00. All I can tell you is that it worked for him and me. I only took two or three Zofran tablets during my whole treatment, but I used the oil quite frequently.

∞ Journals ∞

Keep a journal. A friend gave me one when I was diagnosed, for keeping notes about my treatment. I began with writing down the names of all   the medications I was taking, and the addresses and phone numbers of my doctors.

I cannot tell you how many times the medical team asks about medication. I would hand over the book so they could easily make a copy. I also included an expired driver's license clipped to the book, because a Photo ID is required for many tests and hospital stays. Since I did not always carry a large purse, my journal became my best friend. It was also a place to keep scripts for blood tests or scans, and any other information related to my treatments.

I would also make a note of any questions I had for the doctor and write down what he said as soon as I got in the car. You'd be surprised at how quickly you can forget a conversation you just had. Additionally, I have taken my journal to eye and dental care professionals because they also need to know what chemicals you are ingesting. I asked the oncology nurse to write the drug information included with the chemotherapy, and add them to my journal's medication page. Knowing which drugs I was taking was an advantage to my doctors and pharmacist. This process helped to educate me about my vision changes due to the chemotherapy drugs.

I also taped the health care business and appointment cards to pages in my journal. When you need to make an appointment or have a question, having all of this information in one place can definitely save some time.

Because my radiation treatment was sandwiched between chemotherapy sessions, I

could go back to the earlier treatment notes
for instructions for what medications I should
take on the days preceding my current
treatment. I'll explain the chemotherapy
process, as I experienced it, in a later section.
The final pages of this book contain some
journal pages for your convenience.

∞Check-ups at the Doctor's Office∞

As I attend my regularly scheduled
appointments, the phone rings off of the
hook. I figured out the Friend Docs need to
keep current so they can diagnose and
become better patient advocates for the next
male with ovarian cancer (sic).

"So what did the doctor say?" If only I had a
dime for every time I got this question, I'd be
a millionaire.

"Well, he said blah, blah, blah..."

It really doesn't matter what the doctor
said because he's always wrong.

Again, wait for it....

*"Well, isn't he going to send you for testing?
Your doctor concerns me; he should be sending you for
these tests!"*

My only retort is "No, he never
mentioned it, but once again, I will relay your
concerns the next time I see him."

"And that's another thing: I don't think he spends enough time with you. Are you sure you understand everything he's telling you because what I hear just doesn't sound accurate. Maybe you should get a second opinion; something is wrong."

"Again, they pulled cancer from my body; they know it has made a home inside me. What part of this is confusing to you?"

The answer is a plea: *"Please, do it for me. I'll feel so much better if you get a second opinion!"*

Ah, probably not. I'm willing to bet this doctor will also prove to be incompetent when compared to the Friend Docs. It's a no-win situation, so release information sparingly the minute you get the first inkling you have stumbled upon one.

Another type of Friend Doc to be wary of:

They'll ask you a question, you'll give an answer and then they'll argue with you.

"Did he give you any medication for your pain?"

"No, I didn't think I needed it.

HERE IT COMES.

"Yes you do! You need to get on the phone right now and call him. I don't understand why you even go if you're not going to tell him you have pain."

"I go to the doctor because he feels the need to check on me. Pain is part of the process. I have discussed this with him and have no qualms about calling if I feel the need for a prescription. I really *am* that smart."

Talk about a circular conversation!

In conclusion, I know the Friend Docs really mean well, but I couldn't resist poking fun at them by including them in this book. Don't worry; they won't see themselves this way. My secret is safe as to who they are but, just in case they do recognize themselves, I want to reiterate that cancer patients like me are smart enough to understand pain and the benefits of medication designed to alleviate it.

5. Cocktail Hour at Chemo Land

The plus side of my entire battle with cancer? The nicest people I met during infusion. There is something that happens to this particular group of fighters that's very hard to explain. It seems as though everyone's sole purpose during this time is to make someone else comfortable. The night before my first treatment, I had a horrible dream: I walked into a beautiful room where everyone was relaxed, but my seat was located in a dark corner with cobwebs. It was a form of hazing since I was the new one and had to work my way up to a comfort level. It's pretty obvious the dream was a reflection of my terror of the unknown, but a pleasant surprise was in store for me when I actually walked through the door and was greeted by the other patients.

These people have an incredible inner strength. As the new one, it almost seemed to me that their job that day was to ensure my comfort and teach me how to maneuver the imposing wheeled bag holders that are attached to your arm. These mechanical attachments are not forgiving. If you get a little too far from their comfort zone, they'll pull and tug at your infusion point until you succumb to their warnings. You will not be released until you have consumed every last drop the pharmacy has sent for your enjoyment.

Your concoction of drugs range from steroids to give you strength — and possibly some beer muscles — to Benadryl, which makes you sleepy. Since the beer muscles deflate rather quickly, you become rude and fall asleep while the wonderful person who brought you must sit upright in the most uncomfortable chair in the hospital, while attempting to stay busy for five hours or so. This is why I think the care-giver suffers as much as the patient. They sit quietly and never complain. I learned how much my husband loved me as he sat there all day while I struggled to stay awake. My effort was futile once the Benadryl kicked in.

In my experience, after receiving my liquid muscles I quickly became a shark for a couple of days and ate everything in sight. If the surgeon had cut me open, I'd have been horrified as to the amount of food the medical team would find. When the cravings wear off, you do return to eating normally, although I must admit I still have more unhealthy cravings than I ever did before. I'm not sure if the excessive appetite is real or simply an excuse to indulge in chocolate donuts, but I look at it this way: maybe those of us who travel to Chemo Land earn that donut, knowing we are approaching the stage of joint and muscle pain.

∞ The Infusion Process ∞

I can only relate my own personal experience, but I'm fairly certain the general idea applies to all. I'm convinced the Friend Docs will be available to critique any mistakes or inaccuracies in my account of this process, so I apologize in advance for any blunders. Be aware that the first infusion session is very awkward but by the second time, you're a pro.

The session begins with you checking in and signing consent forms until your hands ache. Then you wait in a chair that resembles a dental lounger. Each "cocktail" is made to order, and your arrival sets the procedure in motion.

About an hour after arrival, the pharmacy delivers your sack of goodies. Your veins are the portal for the liquid cell killers. After they hook up your IV and place the sack on the wheeled metal holder, you're free to roam around as you please. They ask that you drink plenty of water before and after infusion, so most of your walking is to the restroom. I called myself **Princess Pee A Lot** as a diversion from the annoyance of having to get up and maneuver to the restroom. You have the option of public or private space during this time. For privacy, they provide a curtain which surrounds the area you're in. There is a television available and a desk table for writing and eating. Honestly, that's about it. You watch the plastic bag drip and when it's finished, they start a new one.

The mixture includes some additional drugs to combat allergic reactions and nausea, and a healthy dose of steroids. I must admit my cocktail was mixed to perfection and I did not have any additional adverse effects, other than those that are expected.

A few patients have told me they receive their treatment in pill form. Maybe the day will come when cancer can be treated as other diseases are – with just a pill.

After the IV is complete you can go home. At first, I was filled with energy and felt like I could take on the world because my steroid muscles kicked in. Unfortunately, these effects are short-lived; within two days, you're dog-tired. Everyone experiences different side effects; therefore, I prefer not to go into mine because it's like comparing apples and oranges.

It's safe to say there is some recovery time, which in all honesty, is not always pleasant. But I'll say this again: it's **DOABLE**. You *can* get through it.

As I progressed through treatment, it became necessary to undergo a blood transfusion, which is why I now understand fully why vampires choose live victims. During a transfusion, blood is so cold moving through the veins that I felt it the entire time. This was probably in the top ten of my most uncomfortable moments during cancer treatment. Let me assure you, there are not enough blankets in the world to stave off the chill. Sadly, a blood transfusion is just one of the times when we're required to suck it up.

Please do not see this as a negative; it's just the way it is. We've all suffered through being cold in the past, and have lived to tell about it. So I reiterate: the discomfort is doable and passes quickly.

Some folks choose privacy when receiving their blood but I enjoyed the company of other patients. I could probably use a cliché about the warmth of the people in the room with me, but when they're pumping that frigid blood into your veins, you could be sitting on the sun and still be shivering. In the end, the discomfort is worth the final result of feeling a whole lot better.

Actually, receiving another human's blood is in some ways akin to the knowledge of vampira; it had a strange and awakening effect on me. I found myself joking about coming to life after receiving the blood and how much of a life force it truly is. Still, it was a bit unsettling and weighed heavily on my mind. I'm very grateful to the donor for saving my life, yet knowing I had a corrupted life source was a little disturbing.

While it was insightful, I could have lived without ever knowing or experiencing these odd feelings. In horror movies, they speak of eternal life fueled by the forbidden fruit of blood and life force, and I guess in a way I had a taste of rebirth. After a few days I started to notice improvement. It was a slow, steady pace of regaining strength but it was well worth the few hours of ingesting blood icicles. Someone joked and asked me if I was considering having a set of fangs made at the dental lab. Without any hesitation, my answer is *"No."* I have no intention of adding blood-sharing to my activities; however, I am curious if my aura has changed to reflect the new life source.

In closing, you've probably noticed I have mixed emotions about the blood. It just felt strange, which is why I probably gave it more attention than it merits. But I survived because of someone's life force, and for that I am grateful.

Now onto another horror movie reference…

∞ Fighting with a Ghost ∞

This is how I try to explain how I feel in the morning when I wake up. It's almost like I have been beaten by a ghostly goon. My legs and arms hurt and my head feels like I've been in the stronghold of Superman. Fun and excitement comes with the reality that no two days are alike. Thankfully, I look good in the colors of black and blue. Since I tend to exhibit this look frequently, I know this to be true, though I haven't a clue as to where these marks come from. They last for weeks now and as they slither away, they turn a nasty green and grey. *Quite attractive!* Consequently, long sleeves are now my friend.

I've also been experimenting with an array of sunless tanning lotions because I am no longer allowed to be outdoors unprotected. Although I have fair skin, I really don't burn easily. They tell me this will change, so I must apply massive amounts of sunscreen. Shopping for these lotions was an adventure due to the fact there are countless brands and types. It was so confusing I decided it wasn't necessary to learn how they work or what they do. I just asked my doctor for a brand name and number. This is definitely one area where I feel no need to learn more.

Sunless tanning lotions mask the bruises and make you look alive. Use them if you're allowed and indulge in the luxury of looking normal again.

∞ Testing ∞

Today's my birthday and guess how it starts? With a necessary blood test – YAY! These tests are the most necessary evil. I never miss them. I'll bet you can guess I have the kind of veins that are impossible to catch and get into, so I walk around with permanent black and blue marks on my arms and hands. I now embrace them as battle scars; they have become my look.

I will not even attempt to name the assortment of tests that may be necessary for you as I am *not* a Friend Doc. Although the ordeal is quite bothersome, it's another feeling of accomplishment when a test is over. This adds to your strength. Usually there are no further side effects, so it's a good time to finish up the day with a little self-pampering.

One day, while watching a TV talk show, I saw a Hollywood type talking about how she would never put herself through the American way of dealing with cancer. She was leaving the country and going for an alternative method. Here in the real world, most of us are bound by our insurance company as to the eligible tests and methods for which they will provide payment, which usually requires staying within the boundaries of the motherland. I've determined this may be a good thing because although I'm constantly hearing about many alternative treatments for cancer, I see very few good results for those who chose to leave the country.

Even if it means being a test animal, it's the medical knowledge and innovation available today. I firmly believe the medical community wants to save us and is doing their very best. Personally, I have met many survivors of the current regular treatment plans but not many who've taken the alternative route. If unconventional methods really work, by all means, share them with the rest of us. We deserve an easy road to recovery too! Well…maybe not if it involves seaweed and cat food.

6. RADIATION TREATMENTS (OR AS I LIKE TO CALL THEM, SAINT ELMO'S FIRE)

The very first radiation appointment was a form of set-up; I was introduced to the staff and advised of the process. I received five tattoo markings, appearing as if they were taking measurements and creating some type of diagrams for future reference. From that point, everything revolved around pre-set procedures and proceeded smoothly.

On my first day of radiation, they took me back to a waiting area in a comfortable, yet intimidating room where was I was supposed to sit and relax. I did the best I could but I smelled the aroma of toast. The first thing that came to mind was, "Oh my God, they cook us and we smell like bread being toasted during the treatment!" I didn't say anything to anyone but the next day when I walked in there it was again, the smell of toast. Now I'm *totally* convinced that the beginning treatments of radiation singe the organs. As I lay on the table with my hands in what appears to be a dog pull toy and my feet bound in a larger version of such a toy, I'm absolutely certain I'm being toasted.

After a few sessions, I finally explained what was going on to my husband, at which he laughed hysterically. After composing himself, he suggested that the most likely explanation was that the radiation room was located above the snack bar, or that someone was making breakfast. After all, it was 7 a.m.; either one of these scenarios sounded perfectly logical. As for me, I wasn't buying it.

But a few weeks later, the toast smell faded. Now I reluctantly admit he was probably right about the breakfast bar but deep down inside, I still think we smell like toast during treatments – ha!

And for me, radiation was a six-week, daily dose on the *Human Rotisserie*. Because it's a daily requirement, it becomes tiresome. Radiation treatments are quite odd. They place you on a table that is just as wide as you are. In my case, a large cylinder resembling an alien UFO appears. My paranoia stokes the irrational fear that this is not a radiation treatment but some sort of alien abduction. The UFO circles the table while you lie there watching and waiting for little gray creatures to start poking their heads through the slots. OK, so here I am, smelling like toast and waiting to be beamed up into an alien world. Let me point out that there really is nothing else to do while you're on the table, which only kicked my imagination into high gear. You're required to remain perfectly still the whole time, so they bind your hands and feet. Since I'm the type whose feet are always moving, this is a good thing.

Now I'm a few weeks in and since I haven't seen any visible changes to my skin, I'm somewhat more comfortable with the whole idea. Don't be fooled by the Friend Docs who tell you radiation treatment is a piece of cake. It's not an easy road. You are expected to be there every day, receive a treatment, then go home and wait for tomorrow. Sometimes I'd arrive home and by mid-afternoon, be totally exhausted. I could never justify this to myself because there are no outward signs to indicate your receipt of these daily laser blasts. But if you take nothing else from this book, be prepared to experience side effects. I really cannot stress this enough. After talking with others in the waiting room I discovered that most experience some sort of weakness or discomfort including loose stools, constipation, and extreme fatigue. I reiterate: fatigue was the worst effect for me.

Radiation can also cause hair loss. If you have already had chemotherapy as I did, you probably won't see any additional loss. I noticed I had a little bit of fuzz on my head during that time and my hair was starting to return. Maybe it was the toasting or the alien intervention?

By now I hope you've noticed I do my best to take a light-hearted approach to a very serious disease. It's my attitude of choice for survival. If I let the ordeal consume me with fear, chances are I'll lose the battle, but if I mentally put it in a tangible place, I believe I gain some control over the outcome through the process of the unaffected mind. I have a greater chance of overcoming this horrible disease. You see, in my opinion the mind has an abundance of healing power we have yet to tap into. I am trying my best to explore this in different ways – remedial at best – but if I'm lucky enough to stumble onto something, I'm way ahead of the game. It may be an "Old Wives Tale" but laughter is the best medicine. Besides, I *am* an "Old Wife."

∞After Radiation, You Just Keep Cookin'∞

I'm sure if I asked the doctor, he would tell me I'm crazy and probably just experiencing hot flashes...well I have a different idea; I think you just keep cooking.

Did you ever notice when you remove boiling water from the microwave how it looks perfectly innocent until you place a spoon or tea bag into the cup and then it becomes a bubbling cauldron, the envy of any witches' brew? I'm thinking our human bodies react in the same way since they're mostly made up of water.

I am constantly hot. My temperature gauge is permanently in the red zone which tends to be embarrassing when you're the only one in the room wearing short sleeves while everyone else is wearing sweaters. I haven't a clue as to why this is happening, but I have talked with others and they are in the same predicament. This surely is a job for the *Friend Docs*.

∞ The Waiting Room ∞

Explain to me why it is necessary for someone to bring sixteen people – including children – with them while waiting for one patient to be seen. This has to be one of the rudest things I've experienced. I walk into the room, which was designed for my comfort while waiting to see the doctor or receive a treatment, and find no chairs available. As I step over children playing games on the floor and look around for a seat, I spot one way back in the corner. Guess this chair has my name on it.

As I carefully plod my way through, I sit down to the sounds of the loud TV and obnoxious game noises streaming from their cell phones. Maybe this explains why I'm not relaxed when I have my blood pressure taken? At some point, someone gets bored and changes the channel to an insufferable television show where the guest is encouraged to air their dirty laundry while cursing up a storm. Everyone on that side is laughing and having a good old time while others are secretly praying for some good medical news or a painless treatment. After what seems an eternity, their patient emerges from the back and they all get up and leave. The silence is calming and I can finally relax.

My point? The patients coming into this room awaiting treatment are very sick. We're not intolerant; we're scared. Since we're not feeling well, we're quite honestly not in the mood for nonsense. In this particular instance, we deserve to be the priority, so be considerate.

∞For the Women of Faith∞

I rely on prayer every day. Although my loved ones pray for me, I also have to ask the Lord for healing and patience. Don't forget to pray for your own healing. When I schedule my appointments, I do not enter them into my calendar as "Check-up with Dr. So-and-So."

Instead, I describe them as "Healing Treatment at whatever o'clock with Dr. X." My positive phrasing is comforting because it changes my perspective; I don't look at the appointment as a reminder I'll be poked, prodded or cooked like a chicken.

These necessary meetings can be and often are deemed as unpleasant reminders by many cancer patients. Don't be one of them…step up your game and use positive words as descriptors for your appointments. From the beginning, I chose to eliminate any uncomfortable phrases. Don't misunderstand: I'm not hiding from reality, I'm *changing* the reality. Since all of these appointments are designed to assist the body in curing itself of cancer, why not approach them in that way?

Here are some examples:

- ❖ *Healing session with the Doctor.*
- ❖ *Curing appointment.*
- ❖ *Check-up on my health.*

It may sound childish but I prefer to view these appointments with optimism.

And if the best you can hope for is remission, then look at it as X amount of days with good health. Cancer patients are psychologically ahead of most people. We've already been diagnosed and we know how to handle the treatments, so the fear of the unknown has long passed us by. Quite often, the unknown is the scariest part of any diagnosis.

Remember, we place our trust in the Lord. Whenever things get too hard to manage, design a mental box named *Things for Jesus to Handle.* Rather than stressing out, place the problem in the box and forget about it for a while. He delivers.

The parishioners of my church prayed many hours for my recovery. And along the way, there was a time when people told me my skin had a glow. I chalked it up to the chemicals but secretly had a feeling I was being healed. From then on, I didn't fear cancer anymore. Prayer is a most powerful tool and I now believe we must look deep within our souls for the strength to move forward. It is through the power of prayer that we find the appropriate survival skills. Don't be afraid, ashamed or embarrassed to pray.

∞ Retail Stores ∞

As a cancer patient, you're usually subjected to the corner boutique for your supplies. Typically, the owners are the only ones working there and at first glance, they appear to be very kind and sympathetic. Be warned: most are there to make a profit. To them, you are a disposable client/customer. If you've been recently diagnosed, they will sell you all kinds of miracle drugs to keep your eyelashes and eyebrows from falling out, or some fantastic shampoo or cap that will keep the baldness away.

Then, when the inevitable happens, they will sell you a different product to shampoo your hairless head and swear to you that it will assist with the new hair growth, guaranteeing your hair will come back quicker, stronger and thicker. I honestly believe if this were true, Hollywood would install chemotherapy chairs and bottles in their salons. Of course, this product hasn't yet appeared in the latest gossip magazine but maybe I'm onto something.

Because I was scammed by these products, I started reading the ingredient lists. I discovered the shampoo contains the exact same ingredients as my shower soap. There is no difference. The miracle potion in a tube did not keep my eyelashes or brows intact. I lost all of my hair in the exact amount of time my medical team told me I would. I was advised to take care of any hair issues within a couple of weeks after receiving my first chemo treatment because I would then notice the beginning of the loss. This happened exactly according to schedule.

Here's my advice about shampoo and gel: Ask your doctor if you will lose your hair because not all chemotherapy causes hair loss. And if someone tells you the shampoo or cold cap worked for them, use your judgment, ask your medical team, and check the ingredients before you buy it.

My words are harsh regarding the disposable customer; however they ring true. I have spent a lot of money on wigs and have found that even with gentle care they will not hold up past a few months. Even though I bought the expensive wig shampoo, my wigs thinned and showed their age. No matter what you do, the bands stretch, the hair becomes thinner and they take on an aged appearance overall.

I do advise getting your wig cut to the same style you wore before your hair loss, but be prepared because this can cause a whole new set of issues. Even if a hairdresser has the correct scissors for cutting a synthetic wig, don't be assured that he or she has the required talent to style one properly. I once purchased a wig that was a little too long with the idea of getting it styled to my own liking. I left the shop with an Amish mullet. The stylist cut my spiky bangs straight across, then thinned out the back in a way that was just right for 1980. It was money wasted because I have never worn the atrocity.

When I mentioned the bad cut to the salesperson/owner of the boutique who recommended her, to my surprise she responded that I was the *ONLY* customer who ever complained about her. To this I responded that we cancer patients don't always have enough good days to come back to your store and hear "I'm sorry but I'm not responsible after the wigs leave the shop."

Luckily, my shop owner handled this for me. We had a nice chat while we worked together to fix the wig. I talked and she cut. I misjudged her and should have said something earlier but, again, we're sick a lot and must save our energy for the task at hand.

But the truth is, we are disposable. If we survive, our hair will grow back and, if we meet our demise we won't be shopping there anymore. Please keep this in mind when you shop for cancer-related items. You shouldn't have to settle, so if you are treated unfairly speak up, and don't forget to relay your experience to the other patients while you're chatting in Chemo Land. They may return the favor and warn you if they hear about a snake handler in town.

On the other hand, after searching around, I did find a reputable wig- and-hat store where I will admit I was treated with compassion. As you can guess, I had trouble coping with the loss of my hair so this was probably more important to me than a pain pill. Decent store-owners are out there; however, you must do some leg work and shop around because there is much more to this than just buying a wig and plopping it on your head. It takes someone special to help you become a *"Lovely You"* again. And I really feel the need to reiterate this: Ask those around you while you are at the hospital where they go for supplies. I found out about my hair-and-wig shop from the Doctor's staff.

∞ Hats and Scarves ∞

Every Chemo Head has them; scarves are the red flag of cancer. I refused to wear a turban and scarf when I first lost my hair, but after many months of wearing what now feels like a helmet, I succumbed and started wearing them in the house. I have not yet ventured outdoors without a pretty hat or wig, but I certainly can understand those who do. I've tried my hardest to look normal, but I did experiment with the scarf look in the heat of summer.

The scarves look beautiful on the models in the magazine, but keep in mind the silk is slippery and will most likely slide off your head. The lightweight cotton hats will fix this and allow your scalp to breathe. Also, take a good look at the models before you buy. Their hair is hidden under the scarf and they do have beautiful eyebrows and lashes. I think it's very unfair that they are using perfect specimens to demonstrate their product, when those of us who are purchasing them have lost a bit of our perfection.

Furthermore, remember that hats do not cover the side area of your smooth head located next to the ear. You'll be advised to wear large earrings but, seriously, they don't cover a thing. They may draw attention away from your sideburn area, but truthfully the wrong earrings can make you look hideous. Personally, I've found pretty hats to be a suitable substitute for hair on warm days. There are no rules, so wear what is most comfortable for you.

∞ Survivors Looking Backward ∞

Be very wary of survivors who want to talk of nothing else but treatment. This is horrifying. I once experienced such a person and within hours I was thinking the worst. Run away as fast as you can without notice, for they will stalk you. They are living in a past without good results. When you come out of the comfort zone of being a patient it is very uncomfortable, but you have to move forward. You cannot live until you tell yourself you're onto another phase of life's journey. Move past all of the unhappiness and pain. Let yourself become new again.

The first step is to realize you are different. You have fought a fearsome battle, and you may still carry the scars. Be proud of your accomplishment as you have saved your own life. This should never be taken lightly. Feel free to live your second life. How fortunate we are that our future is still to be determined! If you live in the past, you'll probably die in the past. Move ahead and live *Life, Part 2*.

∞ You No Longer Fear The Big 'C' ∞

The word cancer is frightening; there is no getting around it. That being said, after you have been diagnosed and treated, you have a different view of the disease. It is an enlightenment of sorts. You feel empowered that you, along with the most wonderful medical staff in the world – our American doctors and medical professionals – have pulled off an amazing accomplishment. Together, you have faced and defeated a terrible disease. Although not all of us are as lucky as I am to be writing at this time, I do feel the need to congratulate and encourage all of those who have fought the fight of their life.

The word "warrior" is bantered about so much it has lost its true meaning. Playing a sport does not elevate you to warrior status. The 80 year-old veteran sitting in the waiting room for his daily dose of radiation is my warrior and the one I look up to. He has fought for his life on the battlefield, and in the silence of his home while fighting disease. He's also the one who encouraged everyone around him, teaching and inspiring all of us to never give up.

Over the course of treatment, I met a man named Bill in the waiting room. We would see each other every day and exchange amenities, but one day in particular, Bill was smiling. I couldn't resist asking, "Why the grin?"

He replied he felt so proud because he'd been able to drive himself to the hospital that morning. That day was *Achievement Day* for him. His regimen was working and he was seeing improvement. This was his battle and he won. When he reached the end of his treatment, he didn't ring the bell – he drove himself home. I'll always remember Bill; he understood the meaning of life's *little pleasures*.

∞ We're Not Lepers ∞

Brace yourself because this is the heartbreaking section. I've checked on many internet boards that deal with cancer and have found that this is one of the most common complaints. I am at a loss as to why cancer patients are shunned by those who preach how compassionate they are. People will *walk, walk, walk* for a cure but will sit on the other side of the church so as not to be near you. We're not contagious, we're not going to sob continuously, and we certainly are not going to ask for your help. We know better.

Living through this part of the disease has been the worst for me. I am no longer included in meetings or shopping trips. I spend most of my time alone or with my husband, who has done his best to be a pseudo girlfriend, but alas he is a man and doesn't understand the variation in make-up and the pleasure of finding the perfect shoes.

Be advised, neither I, nor my *kind* are seeking pity from anyone. We would prefer to be treated as we were before diagnosis but I have learned that this attitude is more common than not, so we'll move on. Just don't be surprised if we're not there anymore when our hair has grown back and we've emerged stronger from the fight.

I've been somewhat tempted on many occasions to ask people if they would have attended my funeral if the outcome had been different; I am positive most would have said yes. Which begs the questions: *"Why not come and celebrate my life as it is now?"*, *"Did I disappoint you by surviving?"*, *"Do you not receive comfort from your friends when you cry to them about your friend who has cancer?"* (Yes, we know about that part too!)

I recognize the actual answer. The funeral is a public display of compassion while the good news celebration is probably just a relief that they do not have to deal with this any longer. I'm certain it was a difficult road for them to travel.

Although society may shun us, friends may ignore us, and children may point and laugh at the bald lady, we know we fought the good fight. We're fully aware that our outcome will in no way depend upon those who avoided us. We'll go to the mall and shop again, find a new hair style (maybe go for an entirely new look) and, as we are searching for our new life, we will wish you and your compassionate friends well and pray that you never experience the loneliness or pain of a horrific disease.

7. REMISSION: AN ACCEPTABLE FINISH IF A CURE HAS YET TO BE FOUND

I understand I will have to be checked for the rest of my life regarding my cancer status. The word "remission" is an acceptable outcome. It means a second chance. As a young child I would often hear that someone died of "natural causes." Thanks to the advances in the medical field, we don't die like this anymore. We now know why, which is the first step to understanding the how.

Researchers are desperately searching for a cure. In spite of their best efforts it may never happen, which is why we must be happy with the alternatives. Whether you are in remission or, as I have called myself, *Decancered*, moving forward is your only option. Wear the victory as a badge of honor and don't be afraid to strut a bit. After all, your accomplishments are elite in the status department!

My purpose in writing this book is not to hurt anyone's feelings or point fingers. There has already been enough of that, so I'm writing to provide and promote understanding. Our personal experiences are rarely discussed, so like it or not, this is it. If you are a patient, my hope is that as you read this, you realize none of it applies to you because you are well taken care of. If this is the case, laugh until your sides hurt. However, if anything does apply to your situation, have the last laugh as you move forward. The ones who neglected you will have to follow you now. You are the survivor! And by the way, the definition of survivor is as follows:

Somebody who remains alive despite being exposed to life-threatening danger;

Somebody who shows a great will to live or a great determination to overcome difficulties and carry on.

How appropriate is this description of US?! What a feeling of Power! Live on, my courageous friends…

∞ Cut Loose ∞

When the strings are cut, the panic begins. When you're advised of your good test results and that this is probably your last appointment for a couple of months, you go home and celebrate. Then you feel frightened.

When I say celebrate, I mean go to dinner with the one who took care of you. There will probably not be a celebration of your good news. My cynicism is showing again but this is probably the neediest time of your life. Since you no longer have the comfort of the medical staff to answer questions, and the others have moved on to the next public exhibit, you feel abandoned.

In my case, I spent a few minutes looking at my calendar book, savoring the empty pages. I had two months before my next medical entry and I was ecstatic – I was on a pseudo vacation from blood tests and examinations!

Although I was frightened to be on my own, I was ready to live again. I wasn't even sure which doctor I would call if I had a problem but somehow that was okay. I was different now. I know things that others will never understand and I was ready to approach choices by adding the equation of mortality. Before cancer, I'd never considered it. It is amazing how quickly you can decide what is important when your mortal life is threatened. I now find myself asking, "If this were the last day, would it matter?" For me it was an exceptional way of prioritizing life choices. Make it work for you, and don't forget we survivors have a huge advantage since we have already faced the *Big C*.

On the way back to normal, my hair started to grow. How surprised and annoyed I was the first time I had to shave my underarms and legs! I'd gotten used to having smooth, hairless legs, but this is the price we pay for ordinary. I would like to point out that my hair is coming back less than what I had. I never had grey hair but I do now, and quite frankly there are some bald spots. I'm hoping this is temporary but I really don't know as of this writing. Hair extensions have become the norm while my hair is growing back. I have bought two sets of human hair pieces and can work with them to cover the thin spots. My hair has come back baby-fine so the clip-in pieces add some volume. By buying human hair I can bleach and color them as much as I want. As time went on the gray left but my hair is still thin. But you know what? It's *my* hair and it looks good on me.

I was blessed with long, thick eyelashes and am proud to say they have returned. Although my eyebrows have turned white, they can be easily colored, so this is not a high price to pay. My skin is still a little dry but my eyesight has been fully restored. Please feel free to pass this information along with the caveat that I am only one case. We are all different so our experiences and results will vary.

∞ The Transition Back to Some Semblance of Normal ∞

As your hair starts growing in its appearance is awful, but always keep in mind, it's yours and it's growing. After about five months I had a one-inch growth that stood straight up. All I can say is, be prepared for the *Kramer* look. I used to laugh at my hair until strands started popping out of my wig. As a peroxide blonde, dark hairs were showing through the blonde wig. I was instructed by hairdressers to wear a bald cap on my head so the hair wouldn't protrude, but I had other plans.

I bleached the hell out of it. I had never attempted to color my own hair but this was the perfect time to experiment since I would have to cover it up anyway. And what a good time I had.

Interestingly, those who had earlier ignored you will start calling again; they'll also be ready to chat when they see you. Ignore them: if a grown woman is incapable of consoling you when you need it the most, she's definitely unnecessary in your life.

Thanks to cancer, I learned the meaning of the word "acquaintance" and, I might add, how to use it.

∞ The Celebration of Life Party ∞

These words are absolutely the most perplexing cancer patients will ever hear. Some very special and important people have these parties, but I really only hear of them and have never actually met anyone who has had one. However, I did feel the need to address the issue. As much as I hate to admit it, by this time most of our friends have long moved onto something else. By now, they have most likely forgotten to even call to see how you're feeling. You are no longer their rallying call for sympathy; you are reduced to normal.

You may become the person who receives the phone call asking for a donation to the cancer fund. After all, you've had cancer so you of all people understand. In their eyes, you've become a wallet. *Please, I am still trying to pay off my own bills and really cannot afford your weekend of camping and walking for the cure.* Although people believe they are doing good work by supporting these campaigns, those afflicted still have the burden of medical expenses for months, if not years. Therefore, don't ask us for money; our savings are depleted.

∞ Miracles and Such ∞

Someone suggested that the disappearance of my tumors was a miracle. My response? Although it was God's will, it was not a miracle. My heart breaks for the person who doesn't receive this so-called miracle.

Although your intentions may be honorable, it could be very upsetting to someone who may not be receiving good news. Keep in mind, not everyone survives and in some cases, they know ahead of time that they may depart this life. Yet they continue to fight, hoping to be cured.

Another cold statement is "God only takes the good ones," leaving the rest of the survivors to feel unworthy of taking up space in the world. Unless of course it's someone they care about – then it's a miracle.

I've come to the conclusion that we as a society have become so repetitious and redundant, we're not listening to our own words. Try to think of something to say that is truly from the heart and doesn't involve political correctness. Kindness is an exceptional gift. I've seen God take the good ones and the bad ones. As a child I was taught, "If you live by the sword, you die by the sword." This old axiom promotes the concept of taking responsibility for your actions, with nary a reference to a life-threatening disease.

People also like to throw around the term "karma." I would probably respect their opinion if I believed they knew the meaning of the word but alas, I'm afraid most don't. I get the impression that some people think there is a giant Pez-like dispenser in the sky, filled with little rectangles of bad luck which rain upon you the minute they perceive you have wronged them. This could result in your misfortune of being diagnosed with cancer – or worse. Since I'm not a student of Buddhism I'm not very familiar with the actual meaning of the term "karma" but I would be willing to bet that it is a bit more complicated than their perception. So, if you throw this word around, be aware that there are people diagnosed every day and it has nothing to do with karma – good or bad.

∞ **Cancer Phobia** ∞

When I looked up this phrase in the dictionary, I discovered it loosely means "the fear of getting cancer." I find that many people suffer from this affliction and as a result, tend to think it's not a good idea to get too close to a cancer patient. Sounds crazy right? Let me tell you, I could not believe the prevalence of this false belief. *In the 21ˢᵗ century, there are actually humans who believe cancer is contagious.*

There are also those who fear the disease so much, they've deluded themselves that as long as they do not have to acknowledge its existence, it won't enter their home. From what I've learned, neither is true. People will watch us and try to figure out how cancer attacked us. They'll always ask you if you smoke, with the underlying belief being if they haven't smoked, they're somehow immune.

News flash: none of us are.

Some of us have lived near factories or airports; most of us have come into contact with lead or mercury. Even now, when I get a twinge or pain that's a little out of the ordinary my immediate fear is, "Oh no, not again!"

For some reason, we're wired to think the worst. Which brings me to my point: try not to overthink it. Enjoy any and all days untouched by cancer. The medical community is doing their best to discover the causes and cures, but if by chance they aren't successful in our lifetime, the chemical treatments are advancing. Some cancers are curable and some can be held in remission, while others are still mysterious. Make no mistake, the American Doctor is dedicated. He or she will continue to pour all of their expertise, knowledge and intelligence into finding a cure for everyone.

∞ Ribbons and Donation Calls ∞

I, for one, have reached my saturation point with Cancer Awareness.

And now for the berating telephone calls and messages to support the walks…

Please refrain from begging us for money for the cause. I am *my own cause*, and I am currently paying for my own treatment; therefore, I have little to spare. I choose to decline by advising them of the urgency of my own situation. Which inevitably results in the following admonition: "You know you have a greater chance of getting another cancer since you have already had cancer."

Well, thank you so very much for sharing!

Is this the prize for becoming a survivor of an unworthy or second-class cancer? I fear it is. And your insinuation only appears to fuel my fear that there's been a noticeable reduction of my worthiness and humanity.

And then there are the tee-shirts....*Save Second Base, F&*# Cancer*, etcetera. This is a serious illness and such irreverence is appalling! I wonder how many people would be interested in wearing shirts bearing slogans like *Save the Fun House*, or *Save the Baby Factory*. Perhaps many would, but as a survivor I'm worth a little more than that. Trendy tee-shirts don't get it done: the medical profession and chemicals make it happen. If someone doesn't survive, it has nothing to do with their willingness to fight.

Cancer didn't kill me this time. I hope I am not found in an alley, assaulted with ribbons but this must be said: Real people need real help, not pamphlets or t-shirts with catchy phrases.

I consider myself very fortunate to have been invited to share in a day with the Lorraine J. D'Emilio Foundation, set up in memory of Lorraine J. D'Emilio by her family. They treated us to a day I will never forget. A small group of cancer patients along with our guests were taken to a Phillies game, where we were each treated like a princess in our private suite. As if this wasn't enough, they also gifted each of us with a luxurious robe for those cold nights recovering; how very thoughtful.

Such graciousness from the hearts of a family who had lost their precious wife and mother can never be explained. It can only be experienced. I am so thankful to have met them. I learned so much that day as I looked into their souls and saw how they were coping with their loss. This family experienced the day-to-day stress and pain that attaches itself to both patients and care givers. They understood the intense feelings of helplessness, moved on, and did their very best to support others whom they had never met. Although talking as a group was interesting, the most important issue for all of us was our baldness. We confessed to looking at each other and wondering if the hair we saw was real or a wig.

Three out of the four of us were wearing wigs and the other one was incredibly proud that her hair had grown back. She laughed and told us when people asked about the regrowth she told them she had it done at the chemo lab. I smiled a lot that day, laughed, cheered, and had a hell of a good time. There was definitely something special going on. Learning how to bestow the enrichment of life can be achieved; the D'Emilio family has shown us the way. The LJD Foundation is a living example of kindness and good will. While they will always grieve their loss, I admire and commend them for touching us with their loving outreach.

In closing these remarks, I strongly advise you seek out positive groups like this because they are out there. Perhaps they could use a volunteer or some other form of support. I'm convinced of their reluctance to approach you, so take the initiative and proactively offer your assistance.

Many good people work in the shadows of the larger national groups by helping a few people at a time. It's the "behind the scenes" effort that is unnoticed by the community but is appreciated the most by the recipient.

∞ Pamper Me, Pamper Me ∞

If you can't find someone to pamper you, pamper yourself. You deserve it. Be willing to treat yourself after treatment or when you're having a good day. I am a firm believer that things can be made much easier if we reward ourselves. It doesn't have to be something big, just something nice. Maybe a cupcake or a new lipstick will do the trick. I wish I had shown this kindness toward myself since I used to come home with a feeling of accomplishment after treatment. I looked at it as healing but I wish also that I had seen it as prize-worthy, since my life was the ultimate accomplishment.

I guess what I'm trying to say is that the battle is hard enough. Why not fight on with an indulgence now and then? Although it may sound superficial, wouldn't every girl love the idea?

Pampering yourself might also stave off the depression blues. Cancer can have the day here and there, so give it those bad days. Save the feel-good days for yourself. If you can pamper yourself, do it.

∞ What I've Learned ∞

I've gleaned many lessons throughout my ordeal and have met some of the nicest people, but I have to admit cancer is truly an emotional roller coaster and, as my husband says, "Not for sissies."

I think the biggest personal lesson comes in the fight for your life. Ultimately, only you can fight this battle. Your doctor can advise you and administer treatment but in the end it's up to you. Soldier On is the best advice I can come up with. Cry when you need to, laugh when you want to, and wince when you have pain. Only by experiencing this yourself will you be able to understand the emotions and hurt associated with treatment.

Another lesson learned is that people can care more for strangers than they do for their neighbors and friends. The closer you are to some people, the more distance they may put between you and themselves. I've learned that acquaintances are more likely to help out than your friends who talk a good story but do not prove to have compassion.

My intention is to be heartless; I cannot bear to think of any other woman having to keep up her own house while enduring cancer treatments. Loneliness and pain surround this disease, but wisdom and strength are nurtured and developed during this time.

I'm sure some of my friends are chatting about this now. And just in case you're thinking I have taken myself out of the equation, I have not. I would probably be just as guilty in my own ways, for I have always been a snob and I know it. But this "Ugly Duckling" is ready to transform into a new and improved version. I will probably move on as I have outgrown the mediocre environment to which I've become accustomed.

As a true survivor, I expect much more of myself. I have put on the gloves, entered the ring, and faced fear, sickness, uncertainty, and death. I have come through it all scarred, but alive and definitely kicking. I am now in the process of "Cleaning out My People Closet." This is a tactic I have used throughout my life to rid myself of burdensome folks who have no interest in me. My attitude always results in their anger but I've learned that nothing is easy. Daily peace and quiet are well worth the effort.

So we will shed no tears for ourselves anymore, we'll move on and take our beloved husbands and family with us on our journeys, where ever they take us......

Maureen Miles Bucci

∞ **MY JOURNALS** ∞

My Current Medications

Medication   Dosage

_____

Medication   Dosage

_____

Medication   Dosage

_____

Medication   Dosage

_____

Medication   Dosage

_____

Medication   Dosage

_____

Medication   Dosage

_____

Medication   Dosage

_____

And don't forget to include a list of the
chemotherapy drugs. They are important to
any other doctors you may see.

Medications required before and after chemotherapy/radiation

Dosage

_____

Medication Name

_____,

_____ days before/after _____
Chemotherapy/Radiation

Medications required before and after chemotherapy/radiation

Dosage
_____

Medication Name

_____,

_____ days before/after _____
Chemotherapy/Radiation

Special Instructions

_____

_____

_____

_____

_____

_____

_____

_____

_____

_____

_____

_____

_____

_____

_____

_____

Maureen Miles Bucci

Maureen Miles Bucci

Dr. _____

Office #: _____

Dr. _____

Office #: _____

Dr. _____

Office #: _____

Chemo Lab Nurse: _____

Phone #: _____

Main Hospital Number: _____

Radiation Department: _____

Maureen Miles Bucci

Don't forget to ask the Dr. about...

Maureen Miles Bucci

Maureen Miles Bucci

A Snobby Girl's Guide to Dealing with Cancer

Maureen Miles Bucci

Maureen Miles Bucci

ABOUT THE AUTHOR

Maureen Miles Bucci was sharing a wonderful life with her loving husband until her world was turned upside down by a diagnosis of endometrial cancer in 2011.

Having lost a sister to this life-threatening disease, she was already unhappily acquainted with cancer – a formidable opponent. However in the aftermath of diagnosis, Maureen firmly resolved to fight her unique battle as though she were entering the ring for the ultimate boxing match – the outcome of which would mean the difference between life and death. While she was fully prepared to struggle and suffer, she was not willing to concede. Along the way, Maureen developed some practical coping methods for both patients and care-givers through the process of journaling, which later became the foundation for *A Snobby Girl's Guide to Dealing with Cancer.*

Thanks to the hard lessons gleaned from experience, along with her refreshing honesty (borne from a genuine desire to guide others through treatment and recovery), Maureen's writing is raw and edgy. She pulls no punches while addressing and answering many of the taboo questions for cancer patients and their care-givers, in order to adequately prepare them to go the distance. Visit Maureen at her blog: www.maureenmilesbucci.wordpress.com.

Maureen Miles Bucci